MW01222007

House Beneath

House Beneath

•

Susan Telfer

HAGIOS PRESS
Box 33024 Cathedral PO
Regina SK S4T 7X2
www.hagiospress.com

Library and Archives Canada Cataloguing in Publication

Telfer, Susan, 1966-
    House beneath / Susan Telfer.

Poems.
ISBN 978-1-926710-02-0

    I. Title.

PS8639.E428H69 2009   C811'.6   C2009-904629-6

Edited by Paul Wilson.
Designed and typeset by Donald Ward.
Cover art: *Earth Angel II* by Greta Guzek.
Cover design by Tania Wolk.
Set in Adobe Garamond Pro.
Printed and bound in Canada.

The publishers gratefully acknowledge the assistance of the
Saskatchewan Arts Board, The Canada Council for the Arts,
and the Cultural Industries Development Fund (Saskatchewan
Department of Culture, Youth & Recreation) in the
production of this book.

you must be ready for the orphan you were.
and the orphan you are must take comfort for both of you.

Pier Giorgio Di Cicco
"The Wilderness is Yet the Garden"

For Peter and Oliver and Henry and Grace . . .

. . . and in memory of my parents,
Kathleen Louise King McKibbin
and
Richard Warren McKibbin

Contents

I • PASTORAL

No Satisfaction

They crouch together under a young tulip tree
in the front yard of their first house,
cotoneaster growing up the freshly painted wall
behind them. It must be about 1964;

they are young – in their twenties. They smile
with their teeth. The Cold War has started.
She has already been sent home from her
teaching job the day JFK was shot. They have seen

The March on Washington on their first TV;
someone has mentioned Betty Friedan.
They are skinny, she in her pressed white blouse,
he in his pressed striped sport shirt, their pencil

slacks. The sunlight splashes off their shoulders
and her knee, pools around them on the grass.
The head of the new puppy who will bite
friends peeks into the lower corner.

Her father cuts out Eaton's Baby Week
ads and mails them to her, but they are waiting.
The baby boom is ending. Did they drop
a corner of their hope in those times?

I was large in my mother's womb when,
on the radio, she heard ground troops
entered Vietnam. She talked to me
on the Ouija board and I spelled out

"I love you." Did I really choose this
tender fragile pair? He was already
learning to mix rye and soda. She was
reading in Dr. Spock to let me cry.

If I Were An Angel

If I were an angel standing behind
you at your starry kitchen table. If
I placed my hands on your heaving shoulders,
blessing you, new mother, your milk
flooding back, and the baby latching on.
Like a lilac bush sending out suckers
even when the mother plant is dead.

"The dishwasher sterilized glass bottles.
I measured powder into boiled water,
just like in Chemistry class."
                                tura lura lura

If I could teach you to hear the breath
of the infant who will grieve your death,
I'd open your heart to my cries. Protect
your immune system from its auto-crimes.
                                tura lura lie

Surrender. Surrender. Surrender.
Over and over a source asks me
plainly – here is your card – Surrender.

For now you're one of the plentiful dead.
Still, all I need is a mother.

Pacific Pastoral

Sometimes I find a passport to a beach fort
that transposes my mind to the key of D,
key of home, a repeated low D
as in a slow pastoral sonata,

where I feel my strength between
two uncombed logs on a beach. The sun slants
through cracks in the grayed driftwood roof
where light unites me with my future.

Wood chips from the booming ground
are transfigured into slices of bread;
chunks of bark are made, by word, into meat;
I make sandwiches for my doll children;
my child-flesh translates into the Mother.

She hangs plastic teacups on nails pounded
into log walls with rocks, in that *logos*
of a place hand-made, like my block towns,
by a universal catalogue of home,
fragment folded in the back of my mind
where I run the length of the beach on logs,
and only once touch my feet to the rocks.

The Lights of Nanaimo

These nights swirl in the waters of my mind:
the oars arc and swoop in ellipses
below the water and above; drip
a succession of overlapping *O*s.

My mom's voice is there, too. She sings
of the cluster of lights across the strait:
The lights of Nanaimo are shining on me
They're shining and shining all over the sea.

She makes me believe it's a radio
song, like hundreds of others she sings –
morning towns and clouds and raindrops.
Now she is the song beyond the buoys.

And the drips still spell the *O* at the end
of Nanaimo, spreading all the way
across the dark amniotic sea
like poured chocolate across Nanaimo bars.

The way turquoise light broadcasts over
water when it's dark on shore. How a voice
will carry across water, still carries
from that rowboat, cinnamon cottage where

still she sits up all night; she untangles
our lines, woven by a circling salmon.
Still she untangles her daughters' fortunes,
overlapping like *O*s written on water.

Dock

Was that the summer of chicken pox or mumps?
My teeth chatter, toes grip at splinter planks,
six years old in a cotton bikini,
dripping ponytails waiting on the edge
of Davis Bay dock, arms in mock dive pose.

I stand immune on the wharf,
count down but I do not jump, not yet.
For a moment see Dad, treading water below
in the cold ocean by creosote pilings,
calling, "I'm right here." Where he was not.

My mother's shadow holds the towels
and the camera – she's not sure what's at stake.
Am I steeling myself for the life
that's approaching: a foretaste of the dive,
then a dark sinking, then kicking hard for the surface?

In this photograph from my childhood
I stand on the old steamer wharf,
the black indifferent chuck below me.
I'm learning to take stock, to turn fear over,
to fathom how there won't be another me.

I balance at the end of the dock.
I balance at the margin of terror.
Soon I'll surrender to a breath-stopping
shock. I stand immune, alone as an orphan,
shoring up the trust to leap into my life.

Trampoline

My mother lay bleeding in her new bed.
On the record player: I Am Woman.

On the tangerine trampoline, I
levitated – all the new ideas
of the world fell into my mind like
shooting stars I watched at night
sleeping out on the canvas mat.

It was a time when so much was permitted:
nudity, free love, riots.

I bounced to feel the coiled springs resist.
I jumped in my mother's old homemade
prom dresses until the hems and waists ripped.

Her doctor told her, "It's in your head."
On the record player: Killing Me Softly.

I wrapped my doll in the dead baby's blankets,
flipped her high in the air until she splat
on the canvas, and I raised her up again.

One jumper at a time. Seat drop. Knee drop.
Pike. Flip like a falling star. I am strong.

Once I jumped naked on the trampoline
belting out, "Hear me roar!"
But the girl next door yelled through the hedge:
"I see you!" – O – I was observable.

I fell from my trance, hands to my face.

Separately, my mother and I wished
for free hearts, under our prayers to be good.
My palms held the scent of cypress and steel,
a smell that wouldn't wash off.

Scavenger Angels

I beheld the scavenger angels' wings
heavy around my bed one night only,
unhidden as my childhood layer
overlapped into maturity,
the way a rainbow is visible
only when rain passes in front of sun.
My dolls could sing. In my parents' old bed
I gazed upon a photo of naked
bodies draped over one another
and felt a tingle of life. A curtain
opened, remnants of childhood unraveled;
wings wheeled around me like paper cutouts.
I still wonder what shards they found that night,
and when it will be safe to return them.

Outliners

The Osoyoos strip was a line we walked
between imagination and our new bodies;
we walked in the dark hot wind
between two halves of a shallow lake
back from mini-golf and pinball
to the motel in our shorts and halter tops.

We walked a line of blood, embroidering it,
unfurling our sensuality
to the peachy wind, to the cars' honks,
counted them, laughed at the catcalls.
We drew a line around each other –
sister, did we know our power then?

We were outliners of the road strip
where we walked in hot wind, in dark,
of the orchards where we were pressed,
of that town's summer desire,
of rules we dodged. We coloured it all in,
sister, with our private torture, our fear.

The Moment

Not his Buddha posture as he stood
against the party wall, his round glasses.
Nor his answer's tone when I asked him
what song was playing: Master and Servant –
like he didn't believe in the old lines.

Not out walking over snowy fields,
when he told me his coat had once belonged
to his dead grandpa who rode a camel
in a war, and I sensed this tender boy
contained gravity enough to hold me,
a desert wide enough for my sorrow.

Nor in my dark room, my shy body blessed,
when, with his joy mantras, he awakened.

But perhaps it was the next morning, after
breakfast in the cafeteria, when
a bell chimed as he told me his last name –
two letters off my dermatologist's –
a name to mend, save face. Again we kissed.
"Give me a new skin. Crack my enamel," –
scraps spun on my internal prayer wheel.
I believed his kindness would let me heal.

Chapman Creek

Last summer they logged in our watershed.
Someone strung a line of prayer flags
across the creek by the highway bridge.

One summer we walked the old logging road
above the creek, threaded our way downhill
through the ravine's waist-deep salal and ferns.

On the banks of that water source we moved
and flowed like the creek on soft moss; you scraped
your knees. We were thirsty – apart four months.

We had forgotten how easy joy is.
I squeeze o squeeze you. I open my shell
and we're born at the beginning of time

on the riverbank, the first flower ever
to bloom on the riverbank. Genesis
at the watershed beneath bearded cedars

who seem to bend their trunks like our vertebrae
curve toward each other, to reach their arms,
clap their hands, dip their boughs in the current.

I remember how the trees bowed down, love,
to dip their crowns in the fresh water,
as you bent over me, to bless our source.

Peace River

When I was pregnant the first time,
and we didn't know what to do with our lives,
or where we belonged, we drove north
through gilt hills of canola
under colossal flat-bottomed clouds
to the river, down into the basin.
I was comforted by cedars and frogs.
We stayed in that damp peace as long as we could,
listened to the croaking, watched
the river head toward the wrong ocean.
Then we packed up and crossed the great divide,
followed another river south, pulled
as if by a current against our wills,
to face what awaited us by the sea.

II • SINKING

Sinking

I.

An intersection in Victoria –
Government and Fairfield –
standing with my husband, our first baby
sleeping in my old pram.
Mid afternoon, six weeks postpartum,
when the world flipped back right-side up. Suddenly
I sank under the pavement with the weight
of parenthood and how we had to do
what I said I'd never do – return
to the broken family business,
be known in that small town
as the one carrying the weight
of being my father's daughter.

II.

I watched *The Piano*
compulsively, sinking with Ada
to the bottom, anchored by her piano.
I felt my gravity drop in my theatre seat.
Stayed down there for a decade, barnacles
growing on my feet. I was immobile.
No, the worst part was not her sinking,
it was the finger she lost,
chopped off for her transgression.

III.

At night my hands are pulled off,
sometimes served roasted to my children
at the dinner table. And sometimes
it is my feet, but new baby feet
have grown in their place. I'm learning to hobble
in my long white dress – is it my eyelet
May Queen dress or my satin wedding gown?
Dried blood on the hem.

Mother Fugue

My breasts are heavy with compassion.
I push my babies up the steep hill
from the beach to the sick house.
My mother lies tangled in feeding tubes
piping a tinned adult formula
by long stem into her closing-down body.
Nothing I say can nourish my mother.

My breasts are heavy with milk.
I push my babies down the steep hill.
We look into the tide pools like my heart –
what's under that rock? – exposed only
at low tide. For a few hours I exist,
then the tide comes in, I walk up the hill,
and I'm engulfed by my mother, the sea.
I never agreed to insert her feeding tube.
Nothing I do can nourish my mother.

My breasts are heavy with scar tissue
and grief. I dream my son is dragged out
on the current. Cries to me in his life
jacket, crushed between two bobbing rowboats.
I write only black dreams in my journal.
My mother lies beached, a hill of tubes.
I return the rock roofs over the crabs
when we're done, barnacled ceilings down.
Some beings I can keep safely harboured.

My mother's breast is cut off.
In that cell shut-down engulfing my mother,
that year of my mother's eclipse,
Mother Moon tugs me to my beach; I try
to stop the low tide in me. Heavy,
lined blackout curtains block the garden view.
My mother will not look out the window.
I do all I can to nurse my babies
with milk and love, though tainted with sorrow.

My breasts are heavy with milk – my release.
I push my babies up the hill from the beach.
Nurse one – he sucks on the side
of my mother's sick bed, deathbed, prison,
as her body is damned, slows, sips
formula through a feeding tube. She wants
me to nurse her; she fires her nurses.
She can't be my baby: my arms are full.
I leave her exposed. I could do nothing
to show devotion to my mother.

ALS

It has come to this: I am trying to find
a hair in your mouth which cannot open.
You pass me your glasses, raise your eyebrows.
No, I don't need glasses, I snap at you.

You are clear cut: a flaming pyramid
of charred black trunks, rippling orange inside,
like hell, like fear hiding under your skin
in your hungry-hollow, death-white face.

I have a front row seat to your burning:
I nurse my baby on the side of your bed
while you struggle with a feeding tube,
Grace MacInnis on your bedside table.

Mom, you have almost calcified into
the rock you wished to be. Looking in your eyes
empties me of all you have taught me of
striving, appearances. Your pianist's,

knitter's hands now claws, jabbing with a pen
the scribbled word 'hair.' Your mind in morphine's
smoky shadow, you know this is not life.
I walk out. Our anger has come to this.

Staircase

I stand at the kitchen sink in my bare feet
that melting July morning as my mother was dying.

I hear the thumps start on the top steps
over my head. Know in that instant

that my baby has crawled up the staircase
for the first time and is now somersaulting down.

Turning from the sink and running through
the hall as I hear his soft body hit each step.

Reaching my hand out to catch his head
above the tiles. Scooping him up in my arms,

my heart bludgeoning through both of us.
Nursing him then as we breathe at last.

I caught him like when he was born in his sac,
that melting July morning as my mother was dying.

Seal

Little boys in the wading pool
on the shady side of the house, five o'clock.
I stood barefoot with them in the cool water,
then the phone rang.

Last night I dreamed the call came again
as though it were new, eleven years past. Still

impossible – this story.
In the room she lay white, white, white,
mouth wide open, eyes wide open. Now,

on the beach, a seal carcass,
blue ribs, fur and flippers, claws –
I stand barefoot by it in the cold water –
all I have to accompany me
into that sealed-up room
as I say, "I'm still mad at you. I love you,"
and trace a cross with my finger
on her cold forehead.
Stroke her stiff hand.

After Her Death

I. At the Window

I'm in the bathroom. Peter says, "There's a face
in the window with a disapproving look."
I look out but don't see anything so
I open the window and look left.
There in the dark is my mother,
clutching on to the edge of the house
with her toes on the roof edge below.
She has that look like when I saw her
just after she died.
She can't turn her head or open her mouth
but her eyes glare at me, she's heading back
toward the bathroom window. I try to close
the window but can't keep her out.

II. Kitchen Grave

My mom has moved her grave into the middle
of my kitchen floor, like a fridge door.
I hope we don't trip on the handle.
She explains now it will be easier
for her to come and go visiting.
She wants to go downtown but wonders
how she can without a coat or lipstick.

III. *Sawed Piano*

She wouldn't give us her piano
even after her fingers stopped moving,
but she left money for another one.
I played "Au Claire de la Lune" until my boys slept.

One of my first dreams after she died:
my piano is sawed in half,
all the music stolen, but the titles
are carefully cut out and stacked,
so I know exactly what I've lost.

Stabat Mater

The spring after my mother died,
when nothing in my private waking life
mattered enough to write down, I heard
a Good Friday Stabat Mater concert
in the church where I had been married.
When I changed seats after intermission,
the violinist became my mother.

"Mom," I wanted to cry out, because here
was the shining matrix who haunted me,
but my throat was on fire, my eyes streaming,
shivers running through me to the floor.

Now when I look back on that dark year,
I see myself lying on a stained
mattress, reading to a son or nursing,
wishing everything for them to be pure,
reading a materia medica, searching
for a remedy for croup, for teething.
Please just one small sweet universal cure.

What We Burned

What we burned in the backyard bonfire:

sympathy cards, one with a vampire
on the front looking like my father;
all her scrawled notes, illegible;
my dad's notes from detox, where he'd gone as she died;
prescription lists;
feeding tube instructions;
messages from doctors;
her unofficial list of which daughter gets what
– didn't matter because he'd already pawned it;

her glamour, her bravery, her passion,
her humour, which didn't waft in smoky
filaments like the rest, but hardened
into black rocks, then after a few hours,
into gold, which we washed off, wrapped and placed
in a drawer until we grew up enough
to hold them, wonder if one day they would be ours.

Rowboat

I'm in a rowboat with my two babies
and husband in the middle of the night ocean.

There's a storm coming. I know the rowboat
is going to break up. This is my
medicine dream before my mother dies.

•

The next summer, I drive past a white rowboat
and, urged by my dream, go back and buy it.

Each evening before the winds of sunset,
I row out deep toward the Trail Islands,
as though rogue currents might rinse away
my grief, or that I might meet her

on the cusp of time in her old rowboat,
leaning into oars dripping in whirlpools,
as her trembling daughters troll, swaddled in dusk,
smoke-smudged cottages on shore.
"Hold your horses, for crying out loud,"
she'd say. "Why look for me here?"

•

My two boys perch in my rowboat's bow,
trailing driftwood, as we lurch along coastlines,
our bodies drifting through days,
sorrow swimming behind like a dogfish.

I look over the boat's edge toward
dark bottoms for her face, the one I see
so often reflected as I stare
into the bathroom mirror for criticism.
Into her gravestone for approval.

She was my mirror, as the purple-shook sea.

Piano

My mother has stayed – a piano –
a weight in my house, my soul, all this time.
She sings only when touched, resonates with
the heartbeats of my pianist ancestors
in the wedding photo I've placed on top.
Her thundering soundboard myelinates
the spinal cord of the house.
Her timbered heart is tight with wires
that sustain the chords that make me cry.
Without her, the house would be empty,
though I pack the walls with books.
I may call her cold, aloof, a drum.
But I know shamanic drumming's power,
how it sinks my frantic head into
my gut, down into the piano bench.
How it calls to the unborn, kicking
at crescendos. How it summons the dead,
unseen behind me when I turn from
the sonata to the warmth at my back.

Venus

O Venus, glowing austere over black cedars –
you know I want to birth my baby
in my own bed. Car windows are rolled down,
cruising to the hospital in warm wind.
Lavender wrapped our wave-wracked wait:
no hint of what's in the garden beyond.
You know what I need: tenderness, a midwife,
a mother. You know how fear warps labour.
You anoint my feet at waters breaking,
unloop the cord from her neck. Now she cries,
no longer blue. A Chopin Nocturne plays.
Born at the first light of dawn, at new moon.
Home – Venus, I glimpse you in the mirror –
round belly and dripping breasts – I'm eclipsed.

Fecund

Let the butter puddle on the blue plate:
my daughter is three days old.
Colostrum-milk in a blue-handled pump
wastes on the dresser. Peachy jaundiced tan
replaces blue birth skin. My mom's been dead
two years. Now I see how no one can
supplant her. In whose play were we actors?
I promise – a generation *sans* harm:
no more hairbrush chases around the house.
A pitchfork turns a nest of baby rats
into the compost pile; a hand drops tent
caterpillars, writhing in the crackling fire.
It was the hurt I wanted to bury, burn.
I swear, anger's dissolved, envy charred.

Weaning Dance

Between your need and my desire was no seam:
breasts, lips, one flesh; suck, suck a metronome.
Those sweet milk years embrace us like a dream.

Your soul slid here one night through hot bloodstreams:
I swear I heard your laugh past chromosomes.
Between your need and my desire was no seam.

Walking pregnant, I parted crowds like a queen,
then shaman-like, squeezed you through a ring of bone.
Those sweet milk years embrace us like a dream.

First days melted butter; you slept in sunbeams.
Skin-on-skin taught your mouth the essence of home.
Between your need and my desire was no seam.

My breasts fed and fed you – they were redeemed
when your body was nourished by mine alone.
Those sweet milk years embrace us like a dream.

My last baby – one day you wanted to wean –
our bodies still resonate in the same tone.
Between your need and my desire is no seam.
Those sweet milk years embrace us like a dream.

Mercy

> Late August, given heavy rain and sun
> For a full week, the blackberries would ripen.
> At first, just one, a glossy purple clot
> Among others, red, green, hard as a knot.
>
> Seamus Heaney
"Blackberry Picking"

Wet summer nights, hot days, laden vines.
I stand in tall grass picking blackberries,
fallen berries staining the soles of my feet
with summer's blood, as from a sacrifice.
Purple double stroller filled with buckets,
children streaked purple head to toe. I've begun
seeing you, mom, leaning up a ladder
off back roads, your long sleeves, picking blackberries.
Remembering you now leaves me undone.
Late August, given heavy rain and sun,

given the right temperature, you filled cupboards
with apple sauce, pickles, jams and jellies.
How you preserved and preserved with paraffin wax,
cheesecloth bags, scalding water, snap-on lids,
the simmering seeded heat of your mid-thirties,
in your high heels, living room jive dancing then.
"Hello, gorgeous," dad would say at the sink.
A sack was strung from the kitchen ceiling.
Bulging with berries, black juice dripped when,
for a full week, the blackberries would ripen.

Then a flurry of pastry and rolling pins.
Look – a picture – a blackberry pie for
a first birthday the month after you died.
I can't bear to glue it in an album –
you were the one who always took snapshots,
sacrificed sanity to keep your story
in order. Were you searching for mercy?
While you swallowed words, sewed quilts, slammed doors,
did what you thought a mother should and ought.
At first, just one, a glossy purple clot

invisible to the eye one Hallowe'en
under your arm as you dressed as a witch.
Then surgery, and I didn't preserve
your wedding dress, your china or silver.
All you tried to save for me tastes sour.
Even your advice has begun to rot.
Now if I could preserve one dark jar,
it would hold mercy, a purple sweetness
to keep on a shelf unfermented, a thought
among others, red, green, hard as a knot.

III • BRANCHLESS TREE

.

Fatherless

Far from rescue.
I listen for a voice at bedtime,
Then you phone again
in the middle of the night, speaking nonsense.

When a counselor asks me to picture
an animal, a tiger appears
in my mind. Where is my mother-warrior
on its back, with weapons in each hand?

I'm weak from chasing toddlers, my hips
still wobbly from childbirth. I can't carry you.

Respectable citizens shake their heads at me.
The drug dealers you welcome into your house,
the crack addicts, eye me at the mall,
imagine what my mother's china figurines
will pawn for. Dining chairs broken. Haven't you
already pawned diamonds saved for my sister?

The ambulance sirens are coyote howls
that shake me at night. Bears prowl our yard,
hop the picket fence, break our apple tree.

Let me walk with my chin up.
Still you pound on my door. Even
if I open it, I am fatherless.

You Were Famous

Among apple towns, logging towns,
fishing towns; among school boards,
hospital boards, chairman of both,
your picture still on boardroom walls,
only man in town with a tie,
first to buy a computer,
first house with a microwave,
first office with an elevator,
only one in town besides the hospital's –
does that still matter to you?
Big house, big spender, big lender,
bloody Caesar drinker, rye on the rocks
drinker. Famous at the liquor store.
Do you know my stomach still lurches
to go in there?
Long talker in grocery store aisles,
and the ferry cafeteria line,
charismatic to strangers,
could even lure your children back and back.
Everyone said forgive your dad, and I did.
Big man in a small town, golden boy
until you drank alone
too many times. Then you became famous
among dealers, users and drunks,
for throwing it all away, yes,
infamous father, even your daughters,
your daughters.

Dogwoods

Ah, the extravagance of waxy dogwoods!
April sunlight's surprise is always dogwoods,

and the forgotten smell of summer salt from childhood.
We drive along this coastal highway, counting dogwoods.

The blossoms opened the week you died.
What was the meaning of confetti dogwoods?

The expected phone call stunned me too,
as speaking of death in the nursing chair would.

Put my sleeping baby down, gently down –
please wait until I get there – you should –

I drove to the hospital, my fear
made ridiculous by flashy dogwoods.

You bloated, panicked, drowning: high tide
in your lungs, your every cell flooded,

gasping for breath. Pulled under
by garbage bags of rye bottles, unfiltered blood.

I'm no more a costumed child in pioneer
rag ringlets laced with tissue dogwoods

spread across your slide projector screen –
with my bike on parade in the neighbourhood.

Yet the day of your funeral, my heart
was crepe, fragile as paper dogwoods.

Funeral Fire

Standing room only in the church. Who wasn't at your funeral?
Drug dealers, doctors, real estate agents, welfare recipients,
accountants, people I'd never seen before, an aboriginal chief,
teachers, church ladies who made sandwiches, your mother,
clients, old hippies, healers, your grandchildren, the users you
loved more than us. I sat in the front row of the circle, hiding
behind a child on my lap. When your cousin spoke, opening
the closet, did anyone notice the top of my head lift off? He
told of what you'd dredged up at detox, and I wanted to stand
up and stop him, but black smoke came and choked me.
It was so black, I couldn't see my hands or feet. I was trying to
say goodbye. Inside I felt wind howl, rip bark off trees, swirling
embers into a wall of flame.

As if I had walked home to find you sitting drunk on the
driveway, bottle in hand, laughing, while behind you the house
was in flames.

The Nail

My dad, though he's been safely stored
in a tiny box of ashes in the ground
for over a year, still terrorizes me at night.
He's hammered a large forged black nail through the heart
of my daughter's doll, the one I sewed by hand.

Pastel Portrait

It took a long time to forgive my dad
for choosing death over us. I found
his portrait at the bottom of a box
from my dead grandpa's house, under layers
of pioneers' photos and water-stained serigraphs.

When I held it, I saw my sons' eyes
looking out from my father's child-face.
Innocent – his aunt's skillful hand
more tender than a camera lens –
those eyes, Irish or Ojibway brown,
that glared at me, and still do through my boys –
when I have to stop myself from slapping
my father, hiding in their brown eyes.

When I held my twelve-year-old father's face,
his soft pastel child's face, pink and brown,
my anger yielded for a minute.
So I framed it, hung it by the piano
where I practice loving him,
the one I never knew.

Lost House

I returned to your lost house for a party.
Still, the decks sprouted arbutus trees
and were surrounded by ocean.

More a boat than a house. I stepped through
the raised panel doors. Shame, once palpable,
still pierced the prow of the house like an iceberg.

I remembered how I was a fallen tree
on the floor of the glass box living room,
floating on Moonlight Sonata, its swelling ocean.

Did you think you held any secrets from this town?
Empty rye bottles sent no message across oceans.
Why did the liqueur cabinet always smell of almond trees?

Wine cellar under stairs, clinking ice cubes
echoed through the house, the sickening smell
of booze. I sensed my fear in the walls of each room.

My children ran laughing from room to room,
as though they were looking for you, as though
your dream house hadn't turned to liquid.

Downstairs they found what was once my bedroom.
Here I learned to hold my head low in this town,
here I learned to be the adult of the house.

Too dark to show my children the ocean
from my bedroom window. That November night
the arbutus trees were bare. Were you there?

The town held no mercy for you Dad,
a man lost at sea, lost in your delusions.
Over and over you left us homeless.

Branchless Tree

There is a tree that can grow no branches.
I peer into a tight alder fringe.

I step through dense ferns and salal –
all that fertility – until, in small clearing,

I find it: the massive trunk.
My eyes crawl up the peeling, wounded bark –

All the branches have been cut off,
but why? I ask a warden there.

People living nearby don't like the leaves.
Ever since the tree was a sapling,

they've applied a solution to prevent
the growth of twigs after they sawed them off.

Apply the poison: stunt the growth.
Every year they smear on toxin,

so even though the trunk is tall,
and still living, it has no limbs.

The forest is full of monsters that I love,
spoke the faceless rooted totem.

IV • HOUSE BENEATH

House Beneath

There is another house beneath my house.
How have I not noticed it before?
It's beautiful and spacious in the way
of old houses. I want to repaint some rooms.
It has two kitchens –
one for summer and a larger one
banked in antique cabinets.
This underworld house is on the waterfront
of a subterranean sunless sea.
How have I not noticed that before?
Beside its solid wood front door –
my own house number – raised on the wall
in black wooden block numbers.
A wooden deck, steps going down to a beach.
Not far offshore is an island.

In one room, an old woman lies dying.
Why have I not noticed her before?
She must move out before I can move in.
I count the bedrooms – enough for my children.
Why don't I move into this buried house?
And why have I not noticed it before?

There is a soul in the basement.
I've never noticed it before.
Yes, one heart chamber is ragged from fear,
but others are heirloom and milk-fed.
My dead mother moves off my comforters;
the furtive sea encloses me –
                                    I become
the subsoil housewife of my sunken self.

Crows

One dark rain-sopped afternoon,
our lawn is scorched black with crows –
a smoky blanket of shine and flap.
The bare oak trees, too, fool-full of hundreds
of crows. I have set my plans on fire.

I shuffle the archetype deck for clues –
Orphan, Student, Mother, Poet, Lover.

They caw and caw – what is their message?

Dive, dive
from your tidy nest.
Take it – all you desire.

Hunger

In the terrible dining room I crawl
around our table, my husband.
Strangers are seated, but you've set no place
for me. The table's set with my parents'
"Adrian" white fluted, gilt-edged plates.
I'm on my knees behind chairs, searching
in the sideboard. I find only side plates,
salad plates, antique Crown Derby, all too small.
I'm hungry. I won't get enough.

There is a hunger that is not for food.
Won't you serve me a greater share
of pleasure, make room for my hunger?

Let's replace the strangers at our table.
I can't serve myself as the meal any longer.
Darling, do you recognize me?

Set for me a full plate. I'm hungry.
I crave for you to remember who I am.

Ovulation Song

for Peter

Follow me to the end of the deep dock,
hand in hand and hot wind, full moon over
Penticton shining its wide watery
path to us, then kiss me deep, no
Presbyterian kiss, a kiss echoing
like a long-held choir note, my cheeks humming.
Though my skin is almost too hot to touch,
I need cell communion with you. I've sung
gospel all week, I've walked the labyrinth
in moonlight, wind exhaling in the upper
branches: follow me into our hot cabin,
the narrow bed, the children finally
asleep, and emancipate my longing,
dive into my sweetness; I'll flood your shores.

Night Orphans

Where are all the babies I never conceived?
Night after night the orphans haunt me:
forgotten at the hospital, stolen,
given away to a friend, pleading.

I walk down a long narrow corridor
lined, mile upon mile, with benches,
countless children sitting on them waiting
like puppies, some wiggly, some still.

I walk past many squirming children,
then stop finally in front of a quiet girl.
Would she like to come live with my family?
She looks at me with her orphan eyes, yes.

Another night she stands at the top
of the stairway in pigtails, waving, calling,
"Mommy, don't forget about me!"
They want only to live on Earth through me,

but I've already signed the consent
papers, without my left hand's knowledge,
as though I hadn't meant to forget them.
As though I wasn't lost and orphaned.

Brahms' Sonata in F Minor, 1853

Come with me into the dark theatre
beside where the residential school burned.
Sit with me in the front row, center.
Hear Brahms' minor chords pin you down as if
you were a sheet of foil rattling.
Hear his trios staple you around
your edges. Hear his rubato hammer
your mettle until it puckers, tempers,
then holds fast. You are safe with Brahms, who waltzed
with you in the closed-door living room when
you were sixteen. The German banks were full
of California gold. Industry
chugged. Over here, railroads were laid down,
reserves set up, smallpox blankets traded.
There, his friend tried to commit suicide.
Let Brahms, through sonic intuition,
transpose your pain to F major coda,
leave you shining and bursting and held in place.

Lunch, Not With My Mother

Let's say I ate lunch, not with my mother,
not with my memory of her, nor
even her image, imagined, but
with the essence of my mother, she
as light as a spider on a spoon.

Let's say our conversation was not
a long list of everything she'd missed,
but homeopathic, like all angel
conversations. Let's say she listened
to a few silent, salient wisps:

You have a granddaughter. Who loves to dance
as you did. Who is a lot like you were.

She let the news sink under her tongue
like a remedy. No need to answer.

Let's say that night she wraps me not in wings,
exactly, but in love, shows me a handwritten
letter about a banquet, I catch
one word – I try to read more, as the scroll
is rolled up by an unseen hand.

Madwoman

Two people in the road waved the first police car down.
No need to panic. I stirred chocolate in a pot, made haystacks
and blueberry pie.

Ambulances arrived, then ambulance helicopters, setting down
on the private golf course. People came out of their houses,
crowded by the roadblocks. Widows I'd never seen before
clustered together, dressed in black. The boys had to detour to
get home from track practice, through the elementary school
field. Saw a victim loaded into a helicopter. Media helicopters
swooped low over the neighbourhood like huge metal
hummingbirds. A column of satellite news trucks from the
mainland rolled off the 5:30 ferry, their dishes aimed at the sky.

We all wanted to know the story: a young madwoman broke
out of the seniors' home with guns she had snuck in, a hand-
gun and a hunting rifle. She hijacked a car, and started to shoot
at nurses, a manager, a vacuum cleaner salesman. I stirred
tomato sauce in a pot, made dinner and wouldn't let the kids run
up the road in case the woman was still shooting. Then snow
fell. No one saw it coming, a stretcher blanket over the whole
town. The police wrapped the block in tape like a gift.

I kept stirring my pots. I felt like I had seen it all before –
ambulances for my mom, police cars and helicopters for my dad.
There was even a shooter. The mother of a grade four classmate
chased her children out of the house with a gun one night.
She killed her son.

A reporter interviewed my husband who was out walking the
dog. I watched him on TV. Through it all, I stirred – the scrape
of a ladle on stainless-steel pots. I didn't even hear the gunshots.

West Wind

Amazing Grace tolls on our wind chime
notes in random order, at any hour.
Spirit of restlessness, stir me from placidness,
Wind, wind on the sea. O hear my prayer.

The lake surface mirrors sky's shades –
sea-green, periwinkle, aqua –
slapped with wide, bleached white caps.

White caps on the lake where Shelley drowned.
White caps on Lake Okanagan the night
Kelowna burned down; you watched the wind
change directions from Naramata town.

Drive my dead thoughts over the universe,
I heard Shelley call from his rowboat,
then more faintly, *to quicken a new birth.*
Last night I dreamed I was in transition,
tried to phone the midwife. O hear my prayer.
Dreams are ceaseless waves across my mind's map.

Milky hurricanes, cyclones, typhoons churn
air across warm waters in great spirals,
stirred up by so many defunct ideas –
the world is ours to use as we want –
and all life's cumulative exhalation
in response, crushes, drowns, thousands.
Yet I cry for a poet drowned
centuries ago. *Stir me from placidness.*

O hear *Earth* awaken – she whistles
her prophesy, fingers in her mouth,
over rust-lichened rocks and whipped sea.

Her great lungs cough and cough.

Crossings

I. *Ferry*

The ferry doesn't wait.
If you're late, you miss it, but I've never
missed the last ferry home.

Speeding, sometimes mine is the last car,
sometimes I stay below
on the oily, rumbling car deck to sleep.

I never dream of a ferry sinking,
though one did in the middle of the night,
up north, dragging down two sleepers with it.

My life is at stake
with each crossing.

II. *Iona*

The Iona ferry ushers us to an island,
beyond the roofless houses of Mull.
We're beyond the brink of continents,
the usefulness of our rail passes,
schedules, and what I can ask of you.

"Last ferry returns in half an hour,"
calls the crewman as we disembark
without luggage or money, or a place to stay.
I need to stay, can't explain why
to myself, so barely whisper it to you.

I finger the fine white sand, sit down
in a daisy-floored, pink stone cathedral
with no roof, with the ghosts of buried kings.
Maybe I'm still too dazzled by your love;
I forget how to express my will.

I want you to deliver me from
my sinking need, yet know how one drowning,
frantic, will clutch at the rescuer.
We endure the last crossing back,
ruled by timetables of strangers.

III. *Night Ferries*

In the bay beside the lost house
we find three ferry docks.
One launches to Horseshoe Bay,
the other two depart to the prayer sites
Naramata and Iona.

Can you fathom how I need to return there?
You're driving toward the docks
with me and our son. "Let's go," you say.

We might as well go now; we're so close.
But our two babies will be left behind!
"Don't worry," you say,
"your sister will look after them."

I know they'll cry.
We're on the ferry, halfway across the ocean.
I'm sure our daughter is crying.
I demand to go back.

iv. *Bridge*

A weeping willow grows beside a footbridge,
so towering it hangs over the crossing,
partially obscuring it. I love this tree.

One day as I go to cross the bridge,
a man with a chainsaw is sawing
the willow down, branch by branch.
I try to stop him but he
has orders to cut the long drooping branches
that obscure the bridge, make a mess.
A new tree is planted out of the way.

The birch is in dry ground – it won't grow.
I love this willow, its arching shape.
He has already cut the branches.
The tree is a disfigured stump and
my crossing is ruined.

In the morning, my husband calls me
to the top of the stairs, tells me
a plane has flown into one of the towers.

The next day I have to take the ferry.
Fear smudges the world like wood smoke.
Will there be terrorists on the ferries,
in the city?

Am I ferrying to the land of the dead?

v. *Princess Louisa*

We zigzagged into the windy continent,
up the desolate reaches past clear-cuts,
to an inlet salty and deep, both warm
and enclosed, at the back of this fjord –

the surprise of hot interior air
mixed with salt – the firs looked like velvet.
I was hoping for a sea change.

What do Buddhists say about desire
and suffering?

At the end, glacial water chattered down
to a creek, but in the photo
the waterfall seems to pour into
the top of my head, which some may call
a symbol of initiation.

I never said I wanted devotion,
just to be heard. Like that night your hands
placed on my shoulders made water flow.

Finding and losing and finding
tenderness again. A landscape I did
not recognize on the ferry ride home.

Goodbye, House

after Denise Levertov

House where we conceived and birthed children,
where placentas were planted in the backyard,
where stairs were rolled down and bones were broken
and the children fell in love with books.
Oak saplings have thickened enough to climb.
Bears in the backyard, in living room dreams,
rats in the attic, gerbils buried next to dog ashes.

In dreams I return to find bearing walls
removed and everything painted kelly green,
boxes of our belongings in our enemy's garage.

Your timber rumbled by their subwoofers,
dirt wiped on your door, your hedges hacked at,
stones thrown at your curtained windows at night.

Even your most fertile apple tree chopped down,
after I dug its hole like a grave in rain
as my mother's jaw locked, as my baby slept.

We abandon you.

We must let go of our dreams for you, house,
and we must let you go as a dreamt place.

House, forgive us – your windows were wet
with condensation as we packed boxes.
Forgive my broken vow never to move
from your rose arbour, your picket fence,
        my once anchored house.

Notes and Permissions

Epigraph: "The Wilderness is Yet the Garden," by Pier Giorgio di Cicco, from *The Dark Time of Angels* (Toronto: Mansfield Press, 2003). Used with permission.

p. 17: "Morningtown Ride," by Malvina Reynolds; "Both Sides Now," by Joni Mitchell; and "Raindrops Keep Fallin' on my Head," by Hal David and Burt Bacharach.

p. 19: "I Am Woman," by Helen Reddy; "Killing Me Softly with His Song," by Roberta Flack.

p. 23: "Master and Servant," by Depeche Mode, 1984.

p. 29: *The Piano*, by Jane Campion, co-produced by Jan Chapman and Ciby 2000, 1993.

p. 33: Amyotrophic Lateral Sclerosis, or ALS, is a disease that attacks the neurons responsible for controlling voluntary muscles; also known as Lou Gehrig's Disease.
Grace MacInnis: *Grace: The Life of Grace MacInnis*, by S. P. Lewis (Madeira Park, BC: Harbour Publishing, 1993).

p. 46: "Blackberry Picking," by Seamus Heaney, from *Opened Ground* (New York: Farrar, Straus and Giroux, 1998).

p. 59: The italicized line is from "How the Late Autumn Night Novel Begins," by Tomas Tranströmer, from *the great enigma: new collected poems*, translated by Robin Fulton (New York: New Directions, 2006). Used with permission.

p. 65: The italicized line is from *A Breakfast for Barbarians*, by Gwendolyn MacEwan (Toronto: Ryerson, 1966). Used with permission of the author's family.

p. 71: "Spirit, Spirit of Gentleness" © 1978 by James K. Manley. www.manleymusic.com. Used with permission.
The lines "Drive my dead thoughts over the universe," and "to quicken a new birth" are from "Ode to the West Wind" by Percy Bysshe Shelley.

Acknowledgements

Some of these poems were originally published in the following journals: "Venus," "Fecund," "Rowboat," "A.L.S.," and "Lunch, Not With My Mother" in *The Antigonish Review;* "Crows" in *Exile;* "Piano" and "The Nail" in *Grain;* and *"No Satisfaction" in The Malahat Review.*

Thank you to Don McKay for suggesting the title of the book, and for many early suggestions. Thank you to George Elliott Clarke, Sue Wheeler, and Brenda Leifso, who each read and responded to earlier versions of this manuscript. Thanks to Tim Bowling, Anne Simpson, John Wall Barger, Gabe Foreman, Ray McGinnis, Clea Roberts, Matthew Evans-Cockle, Oliver Telfer, and Eileen McKibbin for listening deeply to and having conversations about individual poems. Thanks to Karen Spicer for proofreading.

Thank you to Paul Wilson for editing my manuscript with care, insight, and sensitivity.

Deepest thanks to Peter Telfer, my first and last reader, for his love and encouragement.

Susan Telfer teaches high school English and Social Studies in Sechelt, British Columbia. Her poems have been published in literary journals across Canada, and she is the recipient of the Gillian Lowndes Award, which is given by the Sunshine Coast Arts Council to a community artist for demonstrated achievement and growth. She lives in Gibsons with her husband and three children. *House Beneath* is her first book.